BEAR FAIRY EDUCATION

Math for Kindergarten : Workbook for kids

Published by: BEAR FAIRY EDUCATION.
Interior Design by: Pani Palmer, Kentucky
Cover Design by: Pani Palmer, Kentucky

10 9 8 7 6 5 4 3 2 1
1. Workbook for Kids 2. Basic Early Learning Children Book
First Edition

NUMBER MATCH

COUNT THE PICTURES AND WRITE CORRECT NUMBER

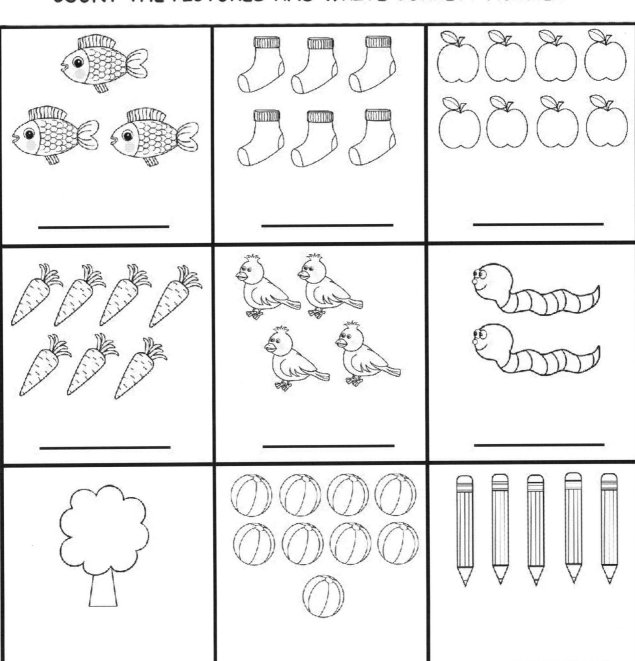

DRAW NUMBERS

TRACE NUMBERS AND DRAW DOTS ON THE 10 FRAMES

2	9	4
3	6	8
7	0	10

COUNTING BACK

COUNT BACKWARDS TO FILL THE MISSING NUMBERS.

DICE NUMBERS

THROW THE DICE DRAW THE FACE AND WRITE THE NUMBER.

Throw 1	⚁	2
Throw 2		
Throw 3		
Throw 4		
Throw 5		
Throw 6		

NUMBER WORDS

CUT AND PASTE THE NUMBER WORD NEXT TO THE CORRECT NUMERAL

1	
2	
3	
4	
5	
6	
7	
8	
9	
10	

five

ten

two

one

seven

three

nine

four

six

eight

LITTLE WORMS

WRITE DOWN THE MISSING NUMBERS ON EACH WORM.

LITTLE WORMS

WRITE DOWN THE MISSING NUMBERS ON EACH WORM.

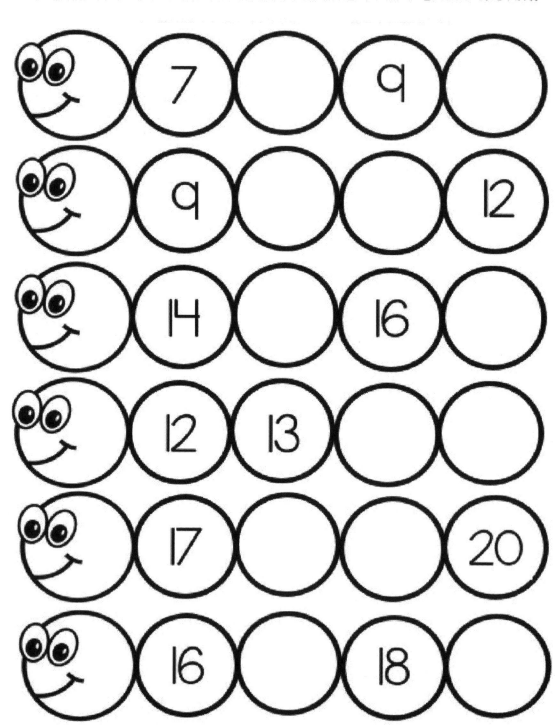

BEFORE & AFTER

WRITE THE NUMBER THAT COMES BEFORE AND
AFTER THE MIDDLE NUMBER

BEFORE & AFTER

WRITE THE NUMBER THAT COMES BEFORE AND
AFTER THE MIDDLE NUMBER

COLOR THE GREATER

LOOK AT EACH PAIR OF MITTEN
COLOR THE MITTEN WITH GREATER NUMBER

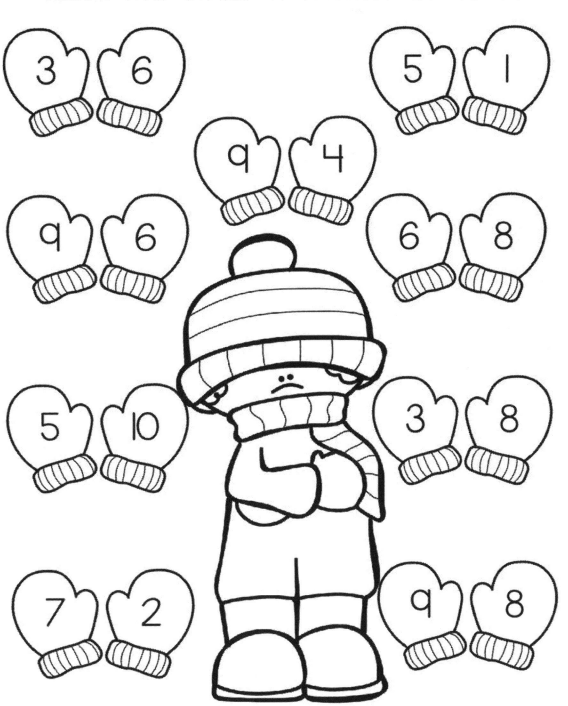

COLOR THE GREATER

LOOK AT EACH PAIR OF MITTEN
COLOR THE MITTEN WITH GREATER NUMBER

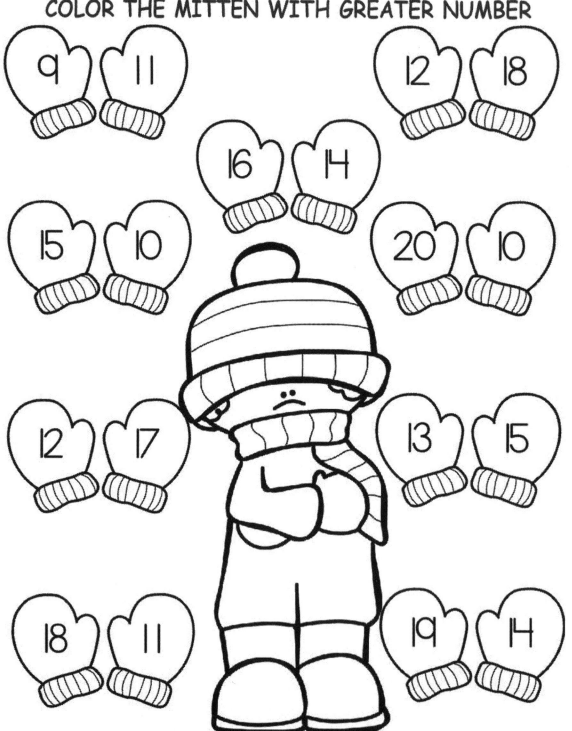

9 11   12 18

16 14

15 10   20 10

12 17   13 15

18 11   19 14

ONE TO FIFTY (1-50)

COUNT AND FILL THE MISSING NUMBERS FROM 1-50

1	2		4	5
6		8		10
11	12		14	15
16	17	18	19	
21		23	24	25
	27	28		30
31		33	34	
	37		39	40
41		43		45
46	47		49	50

ORDINAL NUMBERS

COLOR THE PICTURE IN THE CORRECT ORDINAL POSITION.

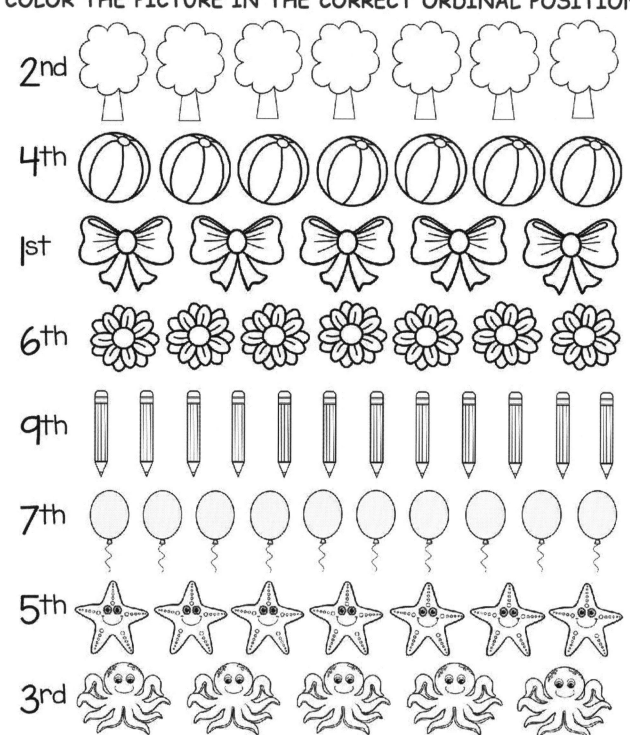

2nd

4th

1st

6th

9th

7th

5th

3rd

IN THE ZOO

ANSWER THE QUESTIONS ABOUT ANIMAL'S ORDER.

dog   snake   lion   cat   pig   rabbit

1. Which animal is 1st? _____

2. Which animal is 4th? _____

3. Which animal is last? _____

4. What position is the pig in? _____

5. What position is the snake in? _____

PICTURE ADDING

WRITE THE CORRECT ANSWER TO THE FOLLOWING QUESTIONS.

🏏🏏 + 🏏🏏🏏	
🐦🐦 + 🐦🐦	
☀️ + ☀️☀️	
🐚🐚🐚🐚 + 🐚🐚	
🍎🍎🍎 + 🍎🍎🍎	
🪥🪥🪥🪥 + 🪥🪥🪥🪥🪥	

COUNTING BY 10

COUNT BY 10'S BY CUT AND PASTE NUMBER IN ORDER.

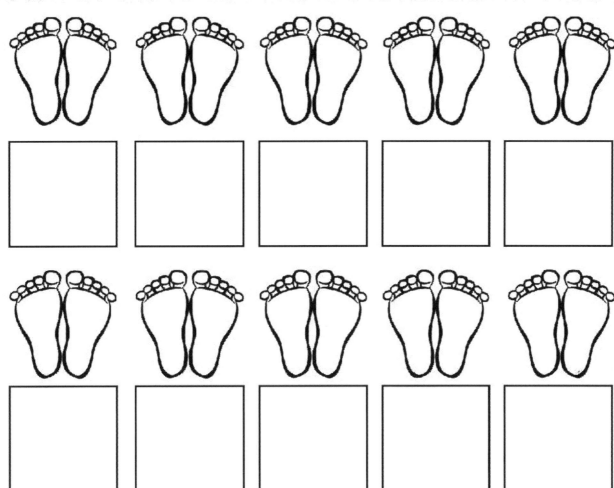

20	90	10	70	40
60	100	30	80	50

DICE ADDITION

WRITE THE ANSWERS TO THE FOLLOWING QUESTIONS.

 2 + 1 =

 3 + 2 =

 3 + 3 =

4 + 3 =

5 + 1 =

4 + 4 =

 5 + 3 =

6 + 4 =

ROLL THE DICES

ROLL THE DICES, DRAW THE FACES AND ADD THE NUMBERS

Throw 1	(dice showing 2 and 3)	5
Throw 2		
Throw 3		
Throw 4		
Throw 5		
Throw 6		

CANDIES ADDITION

FILL IN THE EQUATION AND THEN ANSWER THE QUESTIONS.

☐ + ☐ = ☐

☐ + ☐ = ☐

☐ + ☐ = ☐

☐ + ☐ = ☐

☐ + ☐ = ☐

☐ + ☐ = ☐

TEN FRAME ADDITION

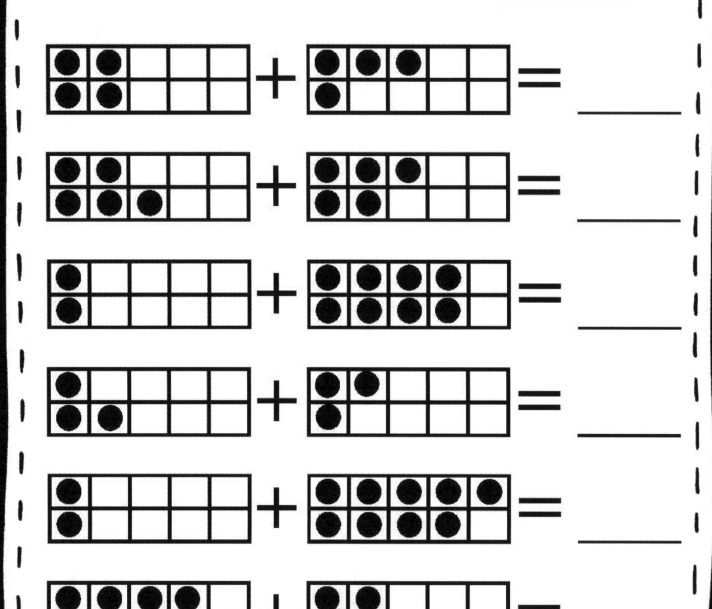

LADYBUGS ADDING

DRAW SPOTS ON EACH LADYBUG,
ADD AND WRITE THE CORRECT ANSWERS.

$3 + 4 = \underline{7}$ $3 + 2 = \underline{}$ $2 + 5 = \underline{}$

$8 + 1 = \underline{}$ $6 + 2 = \underline{}$ $5 + 5 = \underline{}$

  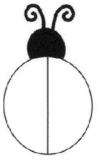

$7 + 3 = \underline{}$ $3 + 0 = \underline{}$ $6 + 4 = \underline{}$

FAST ADDING

ANSWER ALL THE QUESTIONS AS FAST AS YOU CAN.

$6 + 3 =$ _____ $3 + 3 =$ _____

$7 + 4 =$ _____ $2 + 2 =$ _____

$8 + 3 =$ _____ $1 + 4 =$ _____

$5 + 6 =$ _____ $5 + 2 =$ _____

$7 + 3 =$ _____ $4 + 2 =$ _____

$9 + 5 =$ _____ $3 + 6 =$ _____

$10 + 1 =$ _____ $2 + 3 =$ _____

$8 + 4 =$ _____ $5 + 4 =$ _____

$6 + 6 =$ _____ $8 + 2 =$ _____

OVER THE RAINBOW

COLOR THE RAINBOW WITH DIFFERENT COLORS
THEN FILL THE NUMBERS BELOW.

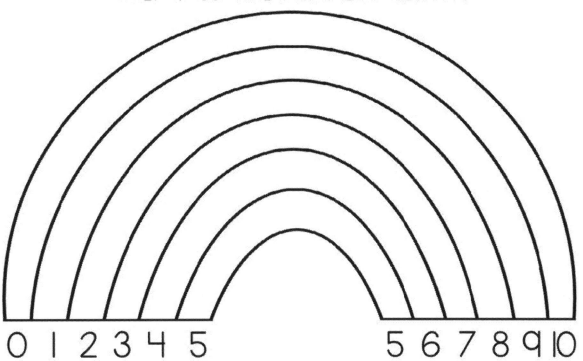

0 1 2 3 4 5   5 6 7 8 9 10

___ + ___ = 10   ___ + ___ = 10

___ + ___ = 10   ___ + ___ = 10

___ + ___ = 10   ___ + ___ = 10

___ + ___ = 10   ___ + ___ = 10

___ + ___ = 10   ___ + ___ = 10

___ + ___ = 10   ___ + ___ = 10

SEA LIFE GRAPH

COUNT SEA ANIMALS AND CREATE GRAPH
REMEMBER TO CROSS EACH ANIMAL OUT
AFTER RECORDED,

6					
5					
4					
3					
2					
1					

ABOUT CUPCAKES

COUNT HOW MANY MORE CUPCAKES YOU NEED TO MAKE 10, WRITE NUMBER IN THE BOX.

 4 + ☐ = 10

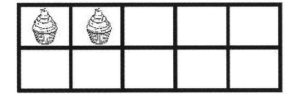 6 + ☐ = 10

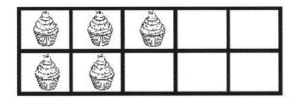 2 + ☐ = 10

 5 + ☐ = 10

1 + ☐ = 10

10 + ☐ = 10

MAKE IT 10

FILL IN THE NUMBERS TO MAKE EACH SEGMENT EQUAL TO 10

PICTURE SUBTRACTION

COUNT PICTURES ON EACH BOX.
WRITE ANSWER TO EACH QUESTION.

HEARTS SUBTRACTION

COUNT PICTURES ON EACH BOX.
WRITE ANSWER TO EACH QUESTION.

4 - 3 = ____

5 - 2 = ____

3 - 1 = ____

6 - 2 = ____

5 - 4 = ____

7 - 3 = ____

8 - 4 = ____

7 - 5 = ____

HEARTS SUBTRACTION

WRITE ANSWER TO EACH QUESTION.

6 - 3 = ___

7 - 2 = ___

8 - 4 = ___

9 - 5 = ___

7 - 6 = ___

9 - 7 = ___

6 - 6 = ___

10 - 5 = ___

FAST SUBTRACTION

SOLVE EACH QUESTION AS FAST AS YOU CAN.

3 - 2 = _____   9 - 8 = _____

4 - 1 = _____   9 - 7 = _____

5 - 2 = _____   8 - 8 = _____

6 - 3 = _____   10 - 3 = _____

5 - 4 = _____   10 - 5 = _____

7 - 2 = _____   12 - 6 = _____

8 - 4 = _____   10 - 9 = _____

9 - 5 = _____   11 - 4 = _____

6 - 6 = _____   14 - 5 = _____

ZOO : CUT AND PASTE

Write the answer to the subtraction questions.

5 - 2 = ☐

4 - 2 = ☐

8 - 4 = ☐

6 - 5 = ☐

9 - 2 = ☐

7 - 2 = ☐

6 - 3 = ☐

✂ -

| 1 | 3 | 5 | 4 | 7 | 2 | 3 |

WORD PROBLEM

Read it:

I had 2 fish and then mom bought me 3 more. How many fish do I have altogether?

Draw it:

Answer it:

WORD PROBLEM

Read it:

The penguin had 4 snowballs and then it made 5 more. How many snowballs did the penguin have altogether?

Draw it:

Answer it:

WORD PROBLEM

Read it:

Jan had 5 balloons but then 3 of them popped. How many balloons does she have left?

Draw it:

Answer it:

WORD PROBLEM

Read it:

I had 9 pieces of candy but then I gave 6 pieces to my sister. How many pieces of candy do I have left?

Draw it:

Answer it:

BASE 10 BLOCKS

Write down the number shown by the blocks.

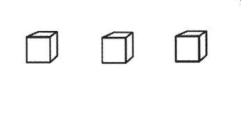
_____

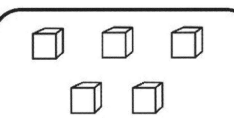
_____

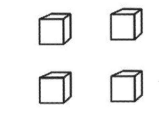
_____

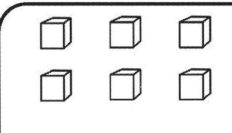
_____

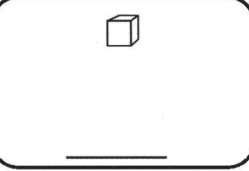
_____

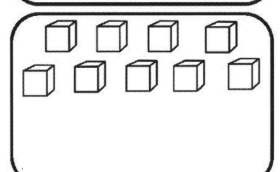
_____

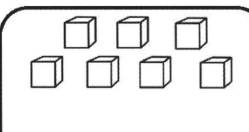
_____

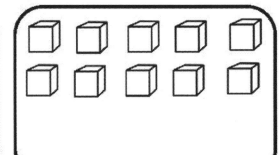
_____

BASE 10 BLOCKS

Write down the number shown by the blocks.

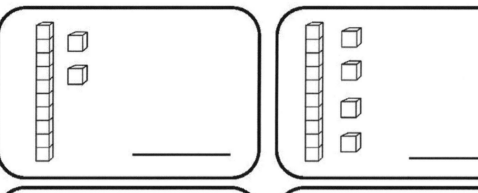

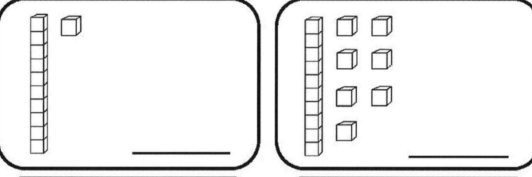

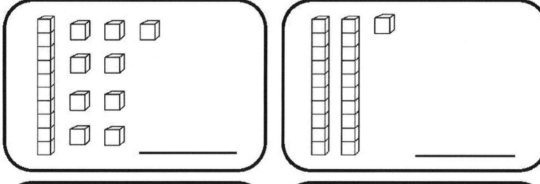

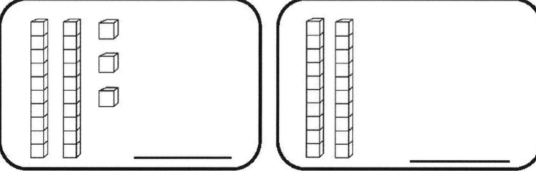

BASE 10 BLOCKS

Write down the number shown by the blocks.

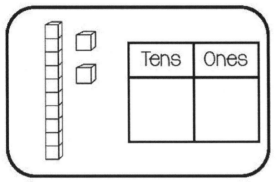

Tens	Ones

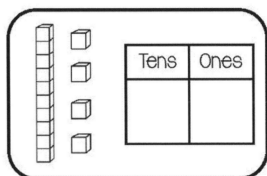

Tens	Ones

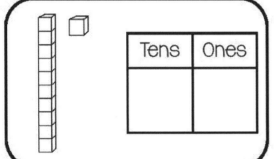

Tens	Ones

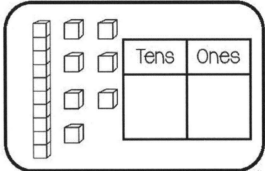

Tens	Ones

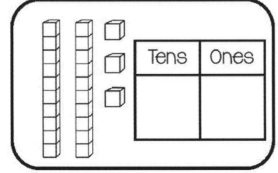

Tens	Ones

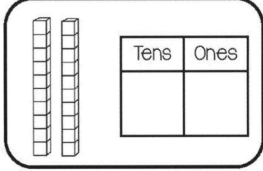

Tens	Ones

TENS AND ONES

Write down how many tens and ones in each number.

6

Tens	Ones

12

Tens	Ones

17

Tens	Ones

4

Tens	Ones

10

Tens	Ones

10

Tens	Ones

19

Tens	Ones

8

Tens	Ones

GEOMETRY SHAPES

Color, trace and draw the 2D shapes.

Color	Trace	Draw
Circle		
Square		
Triangle		
Rectangle		
Pentagon		

SHAPE OF 2D

COUNT THE NUMBER OF SIDES AND CORNERS FOR EACH SHAPE.

Shape	Sides	Corners
Circle		
Triangle		
Square		
Rectangle		
Pentagon		

2D 3D SHAPES

COLOR THE SHAPES USING THE COLOR CODE BELOW.

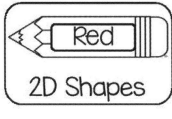

Red

2D Shapes

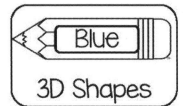

Blue

3D Shapes

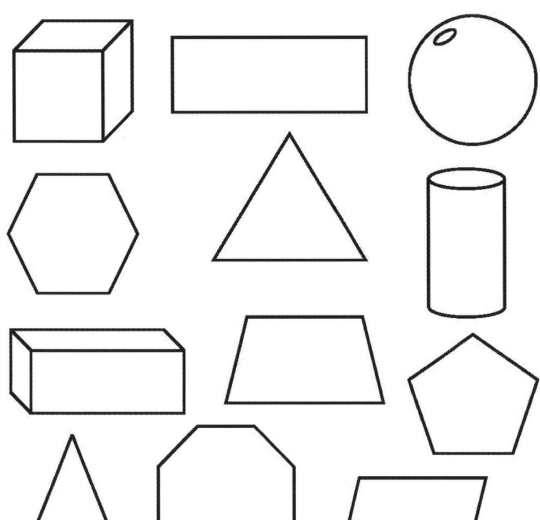

SAME SHAPE COLORING

COLOR THE OBJECTS WHICH MATCH THE 3D SHAPE.

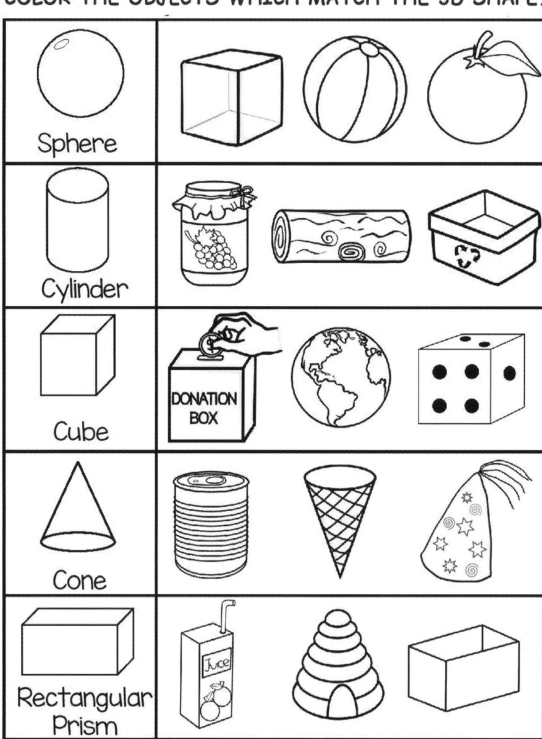

MATCHING 2D

CUT AND PASTE THE SHAPES NEXT TO THEIR MATCHING 2D SHAPE

△ Triangle			
○ Circle			
▭ Rectangle			
□ Square			

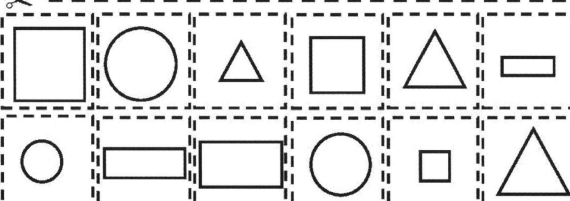

LENGHT COMPARISON

COLOR THE LONGEST OBJECT OF EACH BOX.

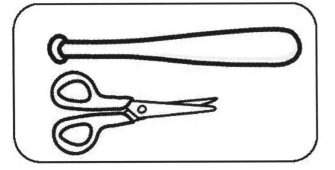
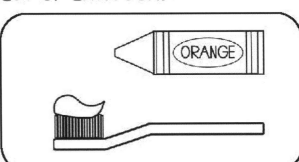
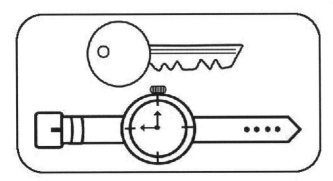

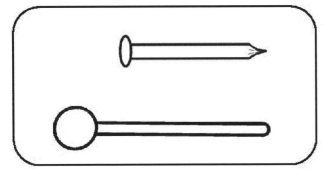
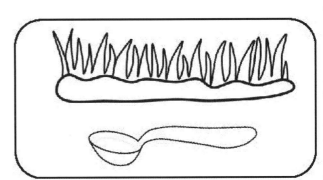

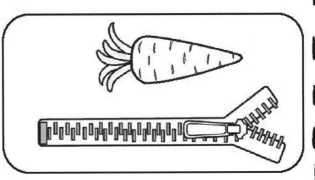

WEIGHT COMPARISON

COLOR THE HEAVIER OBJECT IN EACH GROUP.

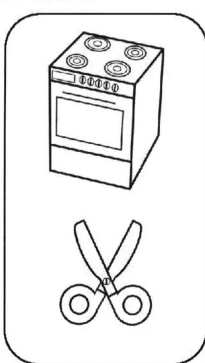

LEFT OR RIGHT

FOLLOW THE INSTRUCTIONS BELOW.

Color the LEFT frog GREEN 	Color the RIGHT hat RED 
Color the RIGHT drum BROWN  	Color the LEFT pig PINK 
Color the RIGHT koala GRAY  	Color the LEFT rocket BLUE 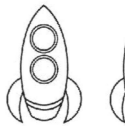
Color the LEFT sock ORANGE  	Color the RIGHT sun YELLOW 

GO TO THE MARKET

Create a graph by coloring in a box for each piece of fruit. Remember to cross the pictures out after you have recorded them.

4 | | | | |
3 | | | | |
2 | | | | |
1 | | | | |

COLOR CODE

LOOK AT THE NUMBER CODE, COLOR THE PICTURE BY THE NUMBER.

1 = brown	2 = yellow	3 = blue	4= green	5 = red

COLOR CODE

LOOK AT THE NUMBER CODE, COLOR THE PICTURE BY THE NUMBER.

| 5 = purple | 6 = orange | 7 = blue | 8= green |

COLOR CODE

LOOK AT THE NUMBER CODE, COLOR THE PICTURE BY THE NUMBER.

| 1 = purple | 5 = orange | 8 = blue | 6= green |

I CAN COUNT

COUNT HOW MANY OBJECTS THERE ARE
AND CIRCLE THE RIGHT ANSWER.

4	6	8

1	2	3

6	9	7

4	3	5

9	8	6

10	9	8

NUMBER LINE

CUT OUT THE NUMBER CARDS AT THE BOTTOM AND GLUE
THE NUMBERS IN ORDER AS YOU COUNT THE SUNS.

1 2 3 4 5 6 7 8 9 10

10	6	8	3	2
5	7	4	1	9

LARGER GROUP

EACH BOX HAS 2 DIFFERENT GROUPS. COUNT EACH GROUP AND CIRCLE THE LARGER GROUPS.

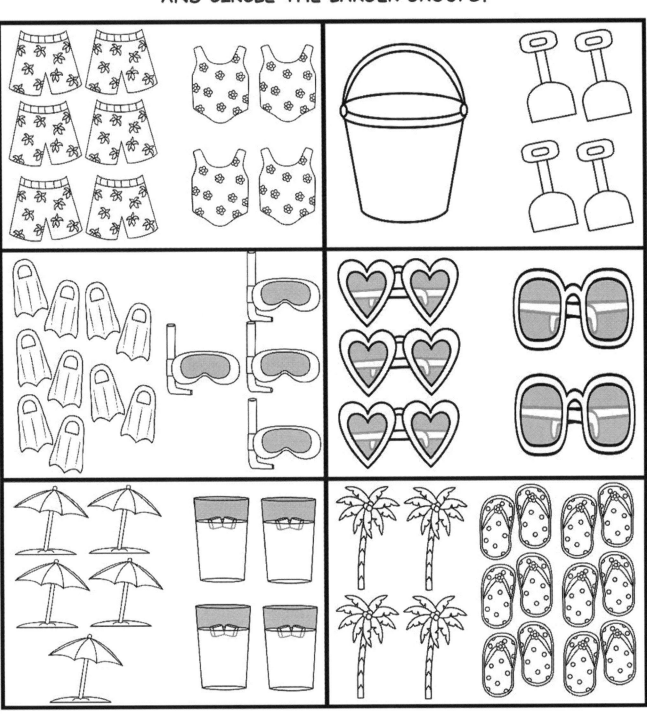

SMALLER GROUP

EACH BOX HAS 2 DIFFERENT GROUPS. COUNT EACH GROUP
AND CIRCLE THE SMALLER GROUP.

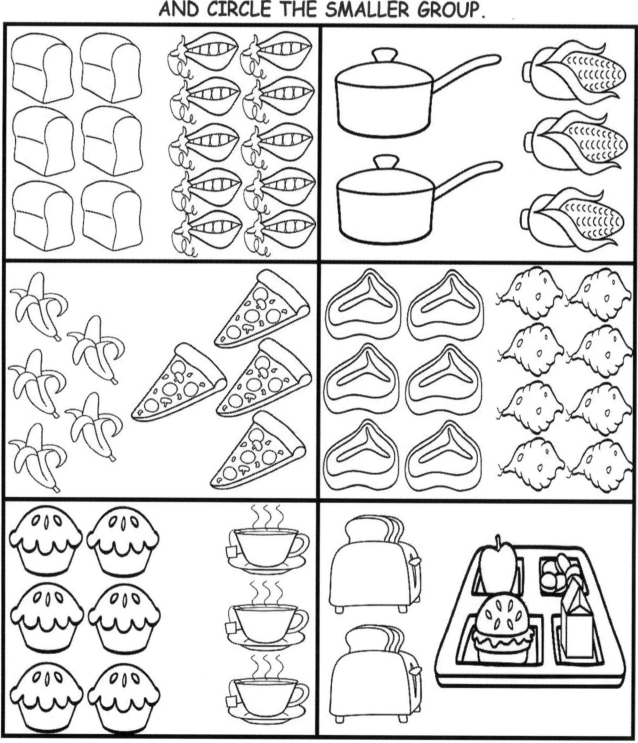

COLOR ME SHORT

EACH BOX HAS 2 DIFFERENT OBJECTS. COLOR THE ONE THAT IS SHORTER THAN ONE ANOTHER.

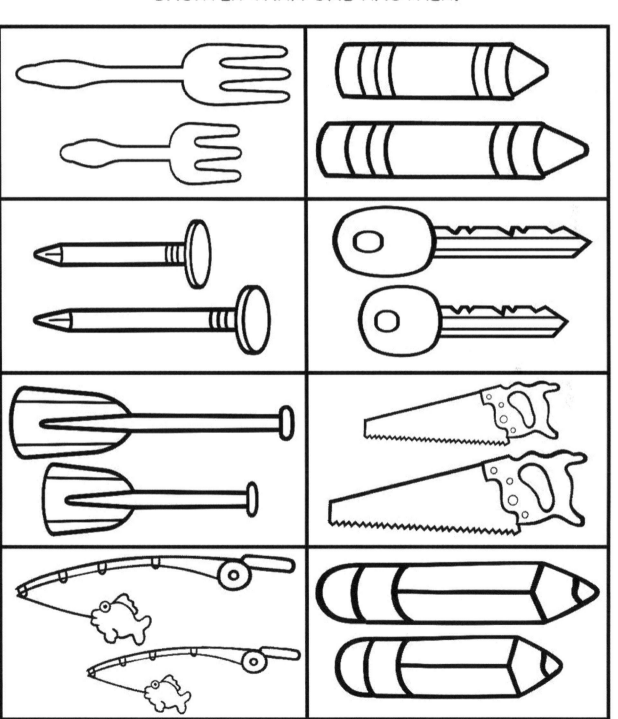

COUNT AND COLOR

LOOK AT THE NUMBER ON THE LEFT AND COLOR OBJECTS.
EX. NUMBER 4 YOU WILL COLOR 4 UMBRELLAS.

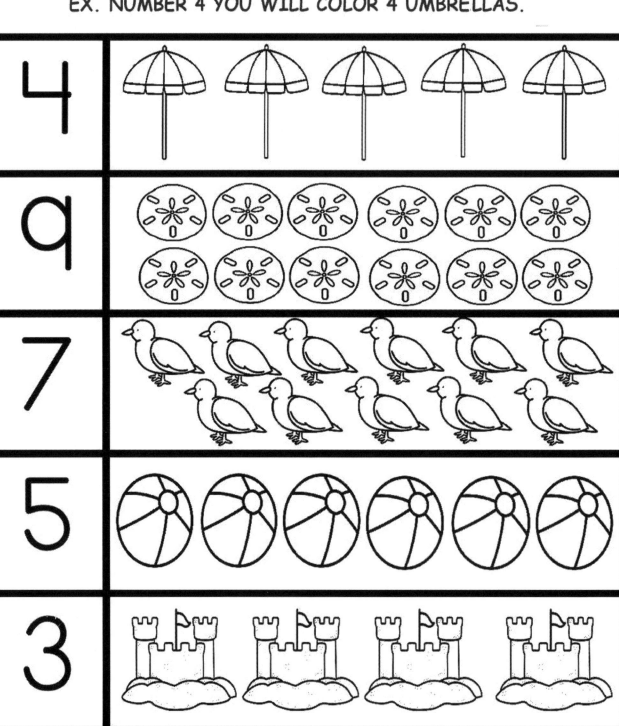

WHAT'S NEXT

LOOK AT THE PATTERN FOR EACH ROW AND CIRCLE WHAT WILL COME NEXT IN THE SECON COLUMN.

READ AND COLOR

READ THE NUMBER ON LEFT SIDE AND COLOR THE OBJECT(S)
EXAMPLE : NUMBER 1 AND COLOR 1 PIG.

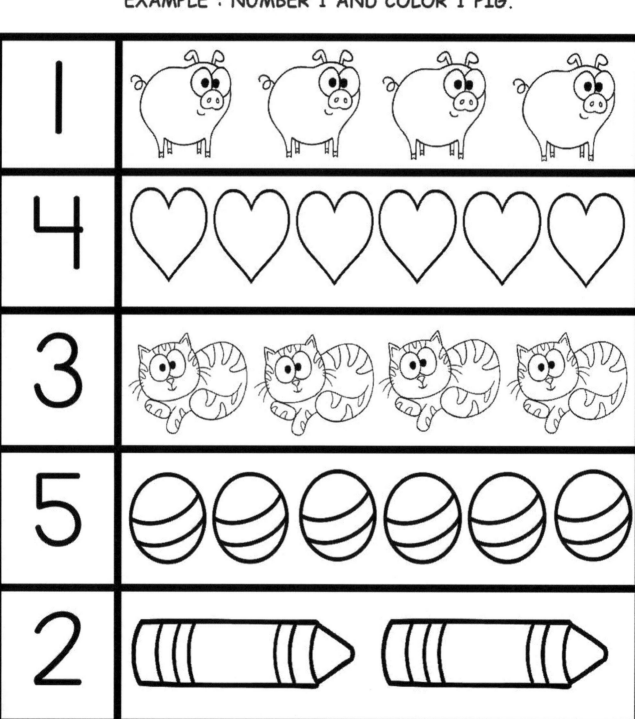

FIND THE NUMBER

LOOK AT THE NUMBER ON THE LEFT AND CIRCLE
THE SAME NUMBER ON THE RIGHT COLUMN.

1	1 4 1 2 1 1
4	6 4 2 4 4
3	9 4 3 3 1 3
5	5 6 3 5 5
2	7 2 5 2 2

Made in the USA
San Bernardino, CA
24 March 2020